Jolly Old St. Nicholas

Illustrated by Andrea Gabriel

Revised by: **Kim Mitzo Thompson, Karen Mitzo Hilderbrand**
Illustrated By: **Andrea Gabriel** Book Design: **Jennifer Birchler**
Publisher: **Twin Sisters Productions, LLC** Song: **Public Domain**
Executive Producers: **Kim Mitzo Thompson, Karen Mitzo Hilderbrand**
Music Arranged By: **Hal Wright** Music Vocals: **The Nashville Kids Sound**

Jolly old Saint Nicholas, lean your ear this way.
Don't you tell a single soul what I'm going to say!

5

Christmas Eve will soon be here. Now, you dear old man, tell me what you're going to bring. Tell me if you can. Please, Santa . . .

when the clock is striking twelve, when I'm fast asleep,

down the chimney with your pack, softly you will creep.

All the stockings you will find hanging in a row.
Mine will be the shortest one, you'll be sure to know.

Johnny wants a pair of skates. Susie needs a sled.
Nelly wants a storybook, one she hasn't read.

As for me, I hardly know, so I'll go to rest.
Choose for me, dear Santa Claus, what you think is best!

Write or draw what you hope Santa will bring you on Christmas Eve.